# FRESH THOUGHTS

## By

## Douglas Moore Jr.

ISBN: 1-4107-9076-2 (e-book)
ISBN: 1-4107-9077-0 (Paperback)
ISBN: 1-4107-9078-9 (Dust Jacket)

Library of Congress Control Number:  2003095861

This book is printed on acid free paper.

Printed in the United States of America
Bloomington, IN

1stBooks - rev. 10/30/03

A portion of the Proceeds from FRESH THOUGHTS will go to the Genesis Fund to assist in providing care for children with Birth Defects

# ACKNOWLEDGEMENTS

This project had been in the works for quite some time and I know this could not of been completed without the support and encouragement from the following:

First off, I have to thank God for staying with me through the ups and downs that life can bring. Without God, I could of never of made it this far to reach this dream of completing my first book of poetry.

My parents- Douglas Moore Sr and Patricia Moore for bringing me into this world and encouraging me to express my mind in the most creative fashion.

Grandma (RIP)-hope you are looking down on me because I miss you lots. The poem "Reflection on a Phenomenal Woman" shows the love I have for you.
Granddaddy- you are the coolest grandfather in the world and I hope I can be as great as you are when I am older.

Aunt Juanita (RIP)- your positive outlook on life kept me focused even when the chips were down and I miss you.

My brother Justin Moore, we have gone through life as brothers and best friends man, but without your support, this book would stayed a dream and not a reality. Thanks for always believing in me and supporting me through the good and bad times.

Thanks to Uncle Jr, Uncle Lloyd, Aunt Pandora, Uncle James (RIP), Aunt Pam, Cousins Ryan, Brianna, Ashley, Jeff, Daphine, Ruth-Ann, Eric, All Faison and Moore family members that have been there for me. My best friend Nate, the definition of a real friend. My favorite soror Lizette, who always has an open ear for me.

Much love to my family of Phi Beta Sigma Fraternity, Inc. and Zeta Phi Beta Sorority, Inc. Especially my Beta Beta Delta chapter at Stockton- Demarkus, Rodney, Julio, Tieyon, Dominick, and Jalal. We made South Jersey a hot spot to be at. Thanks to Lady, Bunchie, Del, Rasheeda and all of my sorors from the Phi Mu chapter. Greek love to everyone, especially all in the NPHC (AKA's, Alphas, Deltas, Kappas, Omegas, SGRho's, and Iota's) who represent their organizations to the fullest.

The whole Stockton College Community, Dean of Students Eileen Conran, The EOF Staff, my professors, and positive Stockton students who showed me support. My finance group at Prudential- Bart, Brian, Mark, Frank and everyone else who has helped me develop there. Thanks to the special people in Massachusetts who touched my heart in different ways, Grisel and Yanira for that sisterly love and Demma for leaving me with deep memories and a drive to complete this project. Thanks to Will, Nicole. Cory, Juwan, Romy, Carlo, Harold, Derrick, Malikah, Horace, Imani, Alex, Ms Beverly, Ms Donaldson, Ms Boon, Zuleika, Ms. Kirsh, Mr. Pezzino, Mr. Salese, Uncle Leff (RIP), and anyone else who I did not mention but played a pivotal part in my life.

The whole 1<sup>st</sup> books Staff- Julie, Elizabeth and everyone who helped get this project of mine out there. This is the start of a good relationship, so let's make push it to the limits.

Everyone on Blackplanet, (Tacoma & all Blackplanet poets), Migente and MegaGreek who sent me the supportive emails when I began displaying my poetic thoughts on those spots.

Thanks to the creative influences who inspired me. Maya Angelou (best poet of all time), 2Pac (deepest lyricist), Malcolm X ( a leader amongst leaders), Bill Cosby, Oprah Winfrey, Sean Combs(sets the standard for handling business), and Jennifer Goldberg( a 1<sup>st</sup> books writer).

Finally, my message is to always believe in yourself and even when the odds may seem insurmountable at times, keep the faith and you will be guided to the right path.

## GRANDMA DEDICATION

# Reflection On a Phenomenal Woman

Poetic words for everyone to observe
As I reflect on a phenomenal lady
Who fought through the adversity
During her most difficult days
In the most admirable way
And this stays on my mind
As I take this opportunity to rewind
On one of the great times
She touched my life

Your phenomenal strength was there
When I would feel too weak
To continue trying to achieve
The success I was destined to see
You reminded me to believe
That sky's the limit
And I should never submit

As a result of those wise words
That needed to be heard
I was guided to the right path
To where success would always last

When I reflect on such memories
That was shared between you and me
It puts a smile on my face
Realizing you are in a better place
Where no more pain will come your way
And I believe you are smiling down on me
Anytime I stare at the sky
I can feel our eyes meeting
Letting me know you are still by my side

# AUNT JUANITA DEDICATION

## JUANITA

I remember the day you passed away
It was a little after Christmas in 96
And I couldn't believe this
Had to happen to me
I lost the one person in my family
Who stood by my side
All of the time
Now that you are gone
I doubt I'll ever be able to move on

You taught me right from wrong
And in your heart
I would always belong
Even when others broke me down
You stayed around to eliminate the misery
Instilled a sense of positivity

Which made me realize
The love you brought in my life
Would always stay true to me

Even though it's been several years
Since your death
I still can't put the pain to rest
Which explains why
I continue to shed tears
For the woman I held so dear

I understand you're watching from high in the sky
And I feel as though
Your spirit has provided me
With the gift to write
About the lessons I've learned
The times I've been burned
So I am not saying good-bye
Because there will be a time
When we can reunite
To establish new memories

# Table of Contents

# CHAPTER 1: SEARCHING FOR LOVE

# DEAR SISTA

I have some thoughts that I need to share with you
About how I heard through the grapevine
You said that good brothas like me are a rare breed
And that you cannot find one
Who is willing to fulfill your needs and dreams

Do you want someone who
After a stressful day of work
Will run a bubble bath for you
Give you a massage to relax you

Say some encouraging words
To eliminate the hate you may have faced
During your rough day in the workplace
Put a smile on your face
Make you laugh to show
Pain does not last

Do you want someone who will

*Douglas Moore Jr.*

Love you for more than your appearance
Have an open ear
To listen to the wonderful ideas
Or issues that mean something to you

Do you want someone who can look
Deep into your eyes and soul
And help you realize there is no need
To look any further for the love you dream of
Because there is someone who wants to give you everything
Your heart desires

Dear Sista
Never allow one bad person
To make you believe
Your dream of real love cannot happen
Keep your eyes open
Never lose hope
Because you never know what your future holds

# CAN I BELIEVE

Can I believe
There is a special girl for me
One who will take the time
And try to find
What makes my heart tick inside

And realize all I need
Is someone who will be there
Have more than a few clues
Of what it takes
To make sure a special bond does not break

Can I believe
When I find that special girl
She will understand how
I've made her love my world
The joy she brings to me
Enables her to see

*Douglas Moore Jr.*

How much we are meant to be
Which increases my curiosity to see
If God personally
Sent her to me

I wonder if I start to believe
All the visions I wish to see
Will they become a reality
Which would mean my dreams
Of discovering the ideal girl
Would erase my misbelief
Love is impossible to find
But it takes a certain degree of time
To find the love that suits you fine

# PERFECT GIRL

I never thought I would see the one
That would end my search for the perfect girl
Even before it begun
You were able to make clear the qualities
Honesty, Sensitivity, and Beauty
Which I consider to be rare
And a dream come true
I wonder if you can see
That I wish there was another one of you
Out there for me

I love when I hear your voice
It brings me so much joy
To know how you feel
And that you see me
As someone who keeps it real
You always find a way
To erase my frown

*Douglas Moore Jr.*

Whenever I am down
Which also shows why
You are perfect for any guy
Who has a vision
Of the perfect girl in his eyes

The thing I love about your most
Is that you see no need to boast
About how beautiful you are inside and out
But every person's heart that you touch
Definitely loves you very much
And I would love to get loud
On the fact you are the perfect lady
The one I would dream to call my baby

I hope by reading my views
On the perfect girl
You see she is a reflection of you

# WOMAN OF COLOR

A woman of color
She could be black or latina
Twist or long hair
It really does not matter
Because she steals my heart away
Sets it on fire
By fulfilling my
Mental and physical desires
In my time of need
Day after day
With her unique beauty
That stands out to me
In so many ways
Because she loves me like no other

She is intelligent and elegant
All at the same time
Her mind

*Douglas Moore Jr.*

Shines so brightly
Because it is so deep
That she can speak on
The world's most serious issues
To her views on the newest poem
By Maya Angelou
And that knocks me
Off of my feet
Reminding me
A woman of color
Loves me like no other

She's a mentally strong woman
Who looks adversity
Dead in the eye
Overcomes the struggle
When things seem too tough
Still finds the time
To eliminate my hurt
When things are at their worst
By staying around
Turning my frown upside down

Because she loves me like no other

And I realize her love
Is more precious
Than any diamond or pearl
That I could ever find in this world

# STILL LOOKING

It's been a couple of years
Since you left me dear
But I'm still shedding tears
Realizing all my fears
Are steadily coming true
Since I'm still without you

I'm still looking for you
To walk through the door
And love me more than before

There's this part of me
That keeps thinking
This whole thing with our love being apart
And me gone from your heart
Is one bad dream
That won't go away

*Douglas Moore Jr.*

And no matter how hard I pray
For this nightmare to fade
It continuously stays

Now I just want to know why
I'm still hurting so bad inside
After all this time that has passed by
Since you walked out of my life

It seems as though
All this wishing for you
To come back to me
Is just silly thinking
That has me still looking
For something that has
No possibility of happening

# WHERE DO I GO

Where do I go
When you finally find
The love of your life
And we both realize
There is no time
For you to be by my side
Which leaves me with
The frame of mind
All of my future days
Will be filled with disarray
Since someone stole your heart away

When you were around
I never felt alone
Because you always made me feel
I meant a great deal
And that persuaded me
To ignore the possibility

*Douglas Moore Jr.*

There would come a time
You would look me in the eyes
Explain there was room
For only one guy in your life
Who was destined to be your groom
At that very moment
I could feel a part of me just die

Without you being near
I feel there is no need
To believe in the things
You used to tell me
Because deep in my heart
I knew with you in my arms
Nothing could tear me apart
But now it is incredibly hard
To picture myself moving on
Since my closest friend is gone

Where do I go
Since the woman
Who used to be my friend
Decided falling in love
Was something of a necessity
Failed to think of me

When fulfilling her destiny

She was in my mind, body, and soul
But now I got to know
Where do I go

# AROUND MY WAY

Around my way
I knew a greedy lady
A cheating lady
An insecure lady
Stressing me and hurting me
Was an evil lady
A cold-hearted lady
A lady

So I believed I'd never meet a good woman
An understanding woman
A honest woman
Who in the worst times
Could make me feel things will be all right
A positive woman
A woman

But other places outside my way

*Douglas Moore Jr.*

Have some of the finest women
Some caring women
Some women of color
Who can love me like no other
The caramel complexion women
The women

In another place, there were sweet women
Lovely women
And helpful women
Who went out and did good deeds
Were compassionate women indeed
The women

I finally realize there are good and bad women
Some intelligent women
Some selfish women
I just need to separate the best women
From the rest
Until I find the right woman
My woman
The woman.

# ARE YOU LOOKIN

I'm not looking for you
To make me feel horrible
All I wanna do
Is love you
And give my best
To ease your stress

But if you keep
Taking me for granted
One day I might realize
And open your eyes
To the fact
My love was too good
For you to have

At this moment in time
Our future is in your hands
Please try to understand

*Douglas Moore Jr.*

I wanna be your man
Through good and bad
But you gotta let me in your heart
And forget about the past ones
Who tore it apart

Just tell me
Are you looking
For that special feeling
That keeps your
Heart and soul reeling
Because if you are
Don't look too far
I'm there with open arms

# LADY FRIEND

She showed me so much attention
Without having evil intentions
Tried to relate to the pain
Of the heartbreak that came my way
From losing someone I loved

My lady friend
Has been there
Through thick and thin
And words can't describe
How much I appreciate the time
She spent staying by my side

She made me feel at ease
When I would discuss the lady
Who broke my heart
Apart into several pieces
By reminding me that if my ex

*Douglas Moore Jr.*

Could not recognize
The love I had for her in my eyes
Then she was not worth my time

Even when I would explain to her
My former love never wanted to end
Our tight relationship
My lady friend would say
Then why does she act like
You no longer exist
By carrying on with her life
And complaining all the time
About guys who don't treat her right
When you touched her heart, body, and mind
And I am left with no way to justify
Why my former love would rather cry
Than have a love like mine

# CHAPTER 2: ANTICIPATION FOR LOVE

# UNTIL SHE CAME INTO MY LIFE

I never knew what love was like
Until you came into my life
I can't even lie
My eyes were shook
By your beautiful looks

And after taking the time
To politic with your mind
I had quickly decided
I felt something between you and I

It's crazy because when I gave up
Had enough of
Looking for love
All of sudden
Like the speed of light
You came into my site
It broke me out of
That me, myself, and I mode

That had sharing my heart on hold

I used to imagine in my dreams
Doing the things you and me do
Like the long walks in the park
Talking about our goals
What our future holds
How the love between us
Is built on a sacred trust

I can easily look you in the eyes
Say that I'll always be there
To protect, never neglect
And most of all
Respect you beautiful
Since you made it possible
To bring this side of me
Back to life
That thinks of anniversaries, wedding rings
And so many other good things
Your love helped me see

# HOLDING BACK

There is no need to keep hiding
Any of the feelings you carry inside
Because over this period of time
You have been always on my mind
Day after Day I wish that
Your heart would continue to come my way

You made it clear that we need space
But every time we communicate
And chill at your place
All I wanna do is stay
And explain how much I think of you
Which is something I always seem to do

I need for you to understand
That I am not like the other guys
Who are there for a short time
And then decide to ignore you

*Douglas Moore Jr.*

Without even saying good-bye

I wanna be there when you are stressed
So I can put all your fears to rest
And always give you my best

I know it is difficult to trust me
But in this case you need to see
That I am on your side
Which is why I do not hold back
About you being all that
So tell me if I am the only one
That you always seem to miss
And then the moment will come
When the fireworks explode
With our first kiss

# ANTICIPATION

As I am pacing to her place
I could feel the sweat
Running down my face
Wondering if when I get to her door
And she looks me in the eye
Will I change what
I have planned to say

This girl has been my friend
For so long
Been with me thru thick and thin
But now I got these feelings
I can no longer hide
And the only way
To get them off of my mind
Is to look her in the eyes
And say what I feel inside

*Douglas Moore Jr.*

I'm getting closer to where she stays
And I'm a little afraid
But there is no way to escape on this
This is an opportunity I refuse to miss
So as I take a deep breath
I'm ready to expose my heart and soul
And see what the future holds

I finally get to her door
I ring the bell
She opens the door with that beautiful smile
That drives me wild
But it's time for me to explain
I know either way
Whatever result that occurs
Things won't be the same with her

# GOOD INTENTIONS

You said you have an interest in me
That's all good but I hope
It's for the right reasons
Because I can quickly see
If you are just using me
To make someone else jealous

So don't waste your energy
Playing any games
Because I will see through your ways
If that ends up being the case

You said that you want a man
Who can understand
What's going on in your mind
Be there in your time of need
Instead of bailing out
When hard times come around

29

*Douglas Moore Jr.*

And you see me as the one
Who can fulfill your dreams

But all I'm saying is
This better not be a situation
Where you smile in my face
After sharing your trials and tribulations
But your heart is still in a different place

Because like I said before
I do not play those games
So if this may be the case
I'm walking out the door
My time does not need to be wasted
By a woman who is two-faced

## No Boundaries

You asked me the other night
If our love feels right to me
Because it is everything
You envisioned in your dreams
And you want to see
If I believe we are meant to be

There are no boundaries for our love
You are the only one I think of
The lady of my dreams
You mean everything to me too
There is nothing I would not do to prove to you
That my love is true

There used to be a time when I
Would wonder why a love like yours
Seemed to never be at my door
But I stayed patient hoping one day

*Douglas Moore Jr.*

Someone like you would come my way

And now that you are in my life
I'll never take for granted
Having a woman like you
All I want to do is love you down
Do whatever it takes to make this last
Because I have learned to understand
Behind every strong man is a beautiful, intelligent woman
So I'm making plans for a future for you and me
There are no boundaries on how things will be

# OUR TIME

We have waited patiently for this day
To come our way
And now that our hearts have finally agreed
On building a future between you and me
That won't get torn apart
By pain and hurt
That almost made this day never take place

Seems to me time played a major role
In deciding what our future would hold
Since there were so many ups and downs
For our love to get around
Such as the temporary lack of trust
That caused us so many issues
That needed to be worked through
In order for our relationship to reach its potential

I remember when we both became so frustrated

*Douglas Moore Jr.*

With the games the other played
We were both ready to throw this love away
Because neither one of us would stop playing the games
Since we were both afraid of dealing
With the pain of heartbreak
But in the end something had to give

We both knew the lies and deceit
Had to come to a halt
And we needed to have a talk to decide
If this was worth giving one last try
Before throwing this away
Letting our love go to waste

Right at that moment
We both realized
We've come too far to go apart
And that our time was developing
Right before our eyes

# CHAPTER 3: MY THOUGHTS OF LOVE

# LOVE SONG

Love song is more than an expression
Defining a sacred confession
Which I consider to be a blessing
The words in my song
Mention why we belong
You are all I want and all I need
So allow me to proceed
And complete my best deed

The desire that comes to mind
Is something not to hide or deny
Beyond the days of being immature
The love I carry for u
Is more than a chore
I know you believe and see
That I never want to be released
From a love so warm and free

No way for me to lose sight

*Douglas Moore Jr.*

And not have the ability to treasure
Every time we communicate
The pleasure
Is impossible to measure

Searching for the one slow dance
All I need is the chance
Only two things can express my feelings
My heart and lyrics
Which arise from my spirit within
Enables a deep and rare tendency
To compose the ways your love
Has reached the expectations
Of what my dreams draw attention to

Your love is real and dear
I wish you were here
So I could recite the love song
Which explains how our bond
Can never be matched
At this very moment I miss
The girl whose love is more than bliss

# ALL OF THE TIMES

The times that we shared
Seems to make me aware
That your love cannot be compared
To any of the others out there

The reason behind why I believe that
Stems from the fact
When I reflect
Put your love into retrospect
I come to the conclusion
What we have is more than an illusion

Reminiscing about how we first met
Not for a second do I regret
Opening my heart and coming through
With ways to say I love you

Those were the most natural words

*Douglas Moore Jr.*

That came to my mind
When showing how all the times
Taught me to keep no feelings behind

The lack of hesitation enables me
To define the destination of our love
And explain that it was you
Who answered all my dreams
By causing me to believe
That every second spent with you
Is more than a dream come true

All of the times allowed me to rewind
Reflect on the special love
That has brought me so much delight
Which in a loveless world
Something so precious is difficult to find

My heart knows where to search
When the feeling of loneliness arises
There seems to be no surprise
Your love is very deep
Causes others to see
By looking into my eyes
All of the times we shared
Has brought so much happiness to this guy

# THINKING OF YOU

For a short time
I was a little confused
On why I miss you
But then it hit me
You found the special key
To my heart
That I kept far away
From everybody

Now you're on my mind
All of the time
When I am awake
And asleep in my dreams
You are the first I desire to see

Who would have thought
I could get caught up
In giving play to slow jams

*Douglas Moore Jr.*

I used to never understand

But now I picture my face
In the songs situations
Such as thinking about
The love I made with the lady
Who stole my heart away

Her explaining to me
When we are close
She loves that feeling the most

I used to imagine
That meeting you
Could never happen
But now that we are together
I will do whatever it takes
To show that
You are loved in every way

I think of you so much
My heart twist and turns
After every touch
I hope these feelings
Grow to become deeper
Than anything
We will ever see

# BEAUTIFUL

Sitting down on a quiet day
Contemplating the best way to say
To my strong, intelligent lady
How she is beautiful to me
In a manner no one else could see

You are beautiful to me
For so many reasons
And unless others get to know you
They would have no clue
On the true qualities
That makes my heart sing the tunes
Of calling you beautiful

There is no doubt physically
You are beautiful
With your tanned skin
Lovely lips and hips

*Douglas Moore Jr.*

Along with your pretty eyes
Which catch everyone's sight
Those are the obvious things
That stays in the minds of others
When you cross their path each time

Your beauty stands out to me
Because I've never met a woman
With the ability
To achieve so many wonderful things
Visualized in her dreams

And even though there was adversity
You still made those things reality
Along with having the time
To be there for your family
In their moment of need

They say beauty is
In the eye of the beholder
And even though I am not you
Your beauty is as clear as air to me
But I just wish others
Would take the opportunity
To see why I truly view you
As Beautiful

# I MISS YOU

I reminisce about the beginning signs
That helped me realize
You are the only love of my life
Such as the first time we kissed
The feeling it brought to me
Or the times we called one another
Late at night to say
How much we miss the other

I think about the ways
You put a smile on my face
When I go through the phases
Of wondering if your love
Will always stay with me

But you erase my doubts
By pulling my close to you
Saying the day

*Douglas Moore Jr.*

You placed your heart next to mine
Was the best choice you made
Because the feelings shared between us
Are so deep that when you sleep
All you think about is being with me

Once we crossed paths
It helped me comprehend
The meaning of the line
"Never say Never"
Because you found a way to my heart
I believed was torn apart

But with your persistence
I could no longer
Put forth the resistance
Of opening my mind
To discovering real love in my life

# JUST FOR MAMI

I saw you mami
With a quick glimpse of the eye
I felt these butterflies
When you got closer in sight

I wondered if trying
To say to you
What was on my mind
Was the right thing to do
At this moment in time

But I already knew
I had to take the chance
To pursue you

Everyday we cross paths
I notice how
My heart skips beats

*Douglas Moore Jr.*

I never thought it could reach
And when we finally
Got the opportunity to speak
It was everything
I imagined it to be

All of your thoughts of love
Were so deep
It left me speechless
Convinced me to forget about everybody
And just think of you mami

The way you occupy
Space in my heart and mind
Forces me to stop being shy
About how I feel inside
So revealing the sweet lines
Which compliment you each time
Increases my will to repeat the deed
Of saying things
That puts me in your dreams
And makes it easier for you to see
I do this just for you mami

# HOW IT ALL BEGAN

I remember how everything happened
It was not even in the plan
For you and me to catch feelings
Because in the beginning
You came at me on a friendship tip
With no signs of us wanting a relationship

Just politicing between two fine minds
Who had their hearts broken a couple of times
With no intentions of
Trying that love thing again

Then all of a sudden
Those late night talks changed everything
I began to recognize
Those sweet and sexy qualities
About you that made my heart
Break out of that ice-cold shell

*Douglas Moore Jr.*

And the fact you were feeling me too
Made me start wondering
Are there possibilities of something developing
Between you and me

How this all began
Between you and me
Keeps staying in my mind
Because I've said a number of times
My heart, body, and soul
Is not ready to go down this road

But the way you've touched my mind
And the feeling I get
By looking into your lovely eyes
Makes me realize
I need to put all fears to the side
Because you never know when real love
Might come into your life

# I FELL IN LOVE

I'm trying to figure out
How I could allow myself
To fall in love
When not too long ago
That was a feeling
I no longer wanted to know

But it goes to show
When you don't plan
For something good to happen
Like a twist of fate
It can easily take place

I remember how she touched my heart
Showed me the type of love
People only have dreams of
And somehow I was lucky enough
To share a bond with her

That no one could ever touch
Unless one of us wanted to end
Our tight relationship
That I felt could not be diminished

It's just so strange to me
How things suddenly changed
Because everything was going so good
I never could imagine
Just being stuck with memories
Of how things with
Her and me used to be

# CHAPTER 4: PAIN AND MOTIVATION

# PAIN OF LOVE

At one point in time
I believed love was stronger than pain
But when the one you think of
Takes her love away
Without any last words to say
The pain stays for longer
Than you could ever anticipate

The feeling is difficult to describe
But let me give it a try
Imagine giving all you had
To someone who felt as though
Your love was all she wanted to know

But in the end she left you confused
Had you feeling misused like Bo-Bo the fool
Because she quickly started brand new
By going about her way
Like none of your special days

*Douglas Moore Jr.*

Ever took place

Why am I wasting my time
Remaining in misery
Over a love that has left my life
It's just that the memories keep playing in my head
So it's hard to put this to rest

But I know I can no longer pretend
Our love has not come to an end
So as these tears rain down my face
I realize pain is stronger than love

## THE STORY OF MY EYES

Look into my eyes
You can easily see
All this pain
That exists in my life
From the strain of unhappy days
That took my smile away

All this pain
You can see in my eyes
Comes at a time
When I'm feeling so confused
About what to do
When I wake up
In the middle of the night
With tears in my eyes

The struggle has been so tough
Because I know

*Douglas Moore Jr.*

Much of the pain
Stems from losing loved ones
Who I still can't believe are gone
So moving on
Seems to be too hard for me

Which explains why
The pain that provides
The story of my eyes
May reside for a long time

# ENEMIES DREAM

I know all the nights
That I scream in my dreams
All my enemies' fantasies
Are becoming closer to reality

Because my presence
Causes longevity to their miseries
So by getting rid of
The stress I bring to their lives
Could become much less
In a matter of time

Imagine what the scene
Would be like
If they finally got me
The sigh of relief
Would be amazing
Since their number one enemy

*Douglas Moore Jr.*

Who had the rhymes
Of a mastermind
Before his time

Never showed any fear
Toward those who hated he was here
But fought to the very end
Even when all his so-called friends
Abandoned him

I might no longer exist
But when you reminisce
About the fights
Between you and I
You will not put behind
The fear you felt inside
After dealing with my explosive side

But I should be the least
Of your worries
Because since you killed me
There are memories of my family
Who want to make you a distant memory

So in a matter of time
Your life will be ended just like mine
Which allows our war to begin once again

# I STAND TALL

I stand before you
As a man
Who has gone through
The best and worst of times
In such a short life

But somehow I still find a way
To escape the hate
The lies and rumors
Others try to use to prove
What they say is the truth
And make me fall
Right in front of you all

Rise or fall yall
I still stand tall
Because the negative words
May sometimes hurt

*Douglas Moore Jr.*

But cannot break or shake me
Because I overcome the adversity
When the odds are
Stacked like bricks to
Form a wall to defeat me

I stand tall
Because I refuse to submit
Give in or admit the pain
They brought my way
Was too tough to overcome

Because I will not lose
I will continue to
Never allow them to
Bring me down
Which is why
I stand tall

# SOMETIMES

Sometimes I lose focus
On getting what I desire most
It makes me feel hopeless
Like things can never be right
But something tells me
To keep trying because it takes time

Sometimes I wonder if
Money can really buy happiness
Or just a short term fix
Of how we wish our lives
Could always be like this

Sometimes I look up at the sky
Wondering why
The good ones have to die
And be taken out of our lives
In the physical form

But are able to still
Touch us spiritually and mentally
In our time of need

Sometimes I imagine what it would be like
To fall in love with one lady
Instead of running into so many bad ones
That's supposed to prepare me to appreciate
The right one that comes my way one day

Sometimes I wonder if
People can relate to
The trials and tribulations I faced
On the road I traveled
To become who I am

## "AND I PICKED UP THE PHONE"

I picked up the phone
And listened to the voice
On the other side
Who happened to be
The love of my life
However this time around
I could feel in her tone
That I might end up alone

Who would have predicted

During the course of the call
She would say
She wants our love to end
And maybe one day
It could re-begin

I felt the tears in my eyes

*Douglas Moore Jr.*

While losing site
She wanted to know
What was on my mind

I placed her on hold
So I could get a tissue
To wipe my crying eyes
From the bad news
That made me feel blue
And left in the cold

I continued to cry

As my body shook
With every word she said
All these memories
Of when things were good
Flashed in my mind

The call came to a conclusion
But my tears were not an illusion
And all I could remember
Is picking up the phone
To end up alone

# LOVE STRUCK VICTIM

She has another love struck victim
Who has all the same symptoms
People helped me understand
I once had
When she had my heart
In the palm of her hands

It's strange to actually see
The pain and agony she put me through
By watching her do the same to him

He's blind to what's going on
Because of her kind smile and lies
That are strong enough
To keep him stuck in her web

Where anything she says
Stays in his head

To prevent him from thinking straight
To recognize her evil ways each day

Even if someone shows him proof
That she's a lying lady
Who has done this thing constantly
He still won't believe the truth

All he can see is her beauty
The things she does to please
Bring him to his knees
So he can continue to ignore reality

Reality won't set into his mind
Until the day she decides
To walk out of his life
Leaving him as another
Love struck victim
Sitting wondering how
He got caught up in her web
Like me and the rest

# BROKEN HEART

Time is supposed to heal the pain of a broken heart
But this feeling is so unreal
It is hard to even start
To describe the way this pain
Has stained how I feel inside

Let's just say it's like
Having your heart laid out
And the one you care about
Out of nowhere
Just decides to slice it in half
Without even feeling bad

The broken pieces of my heart
Leave me feeling torn apart
Alone and confused
Not knowing what to do next
To recover from

*Douglas Moore Jr.*

This broken heart mess

# NOT SEARCHING

I'm not searching
For a lady
Who will cause me pain
By playing immature games
That only gets in the way
Of developing a solid relationship

I'm not searching
For a lady
Who complains about
Wanting a good guy
But once one
Come into her life
She says he is too nice

I'm not searching
For a lady
Who has visions of dollar signs

*Douglas Moore Jr.*

The second I cross her sight
Get to know me from the inside
And it will become
Clear to see my personality
Carries more value than money

I'm not searching
For a lady
Who throws around the word love
Know the meaning of it
So there will be no need
To doubt if you really feel it
For the one who believes
He can do everything
To eliminate your misery
And always keep you happy

# HOSTILE

I seem to be the only person
To notice the demons from my past lurking
To remind me of the bad luck
That keeps coming my way
Will steadily continue
Until they notice my mind
And my passion for life dying
Then it will become clear in their eyes
For me to lose hope and blow up inside

Who would of known
That I will never have the chance
To live the life I wished to own
But now I carry this hostility
And a negative mentality
That was caused by my peers
The ones who eye me with fear
Even though they have everything

*Douglas Moore Jr.*

I could only imagine in my dreams

Now I follow this dark path
Which makes others laugh
Because all of my enemies
Always pictured me
Living out my fantasies
But instead I fell victim
To the horrible symptoms
Which endangered my vision
Of visualizing my dreams with precision
So now I stand angry at the world
While my life continues to unfold

# CHAPTER 5: SHOULD THE LOVE COME BACK

# IF SHE ONLY KNEW

I wish I could explain to her
How losing her love
Hurts so much
The times her and me shared
Keep flashing in my head
And it's so hard to put
These feelings to rest
Because she means so much to me

If she only knew
How deep her love was to me
It would be clear to see
Us being together
Is meant to be

The pain that flows through my heart
It tears me apart
Realizing every day that passes by
She is no longer in my life

*Douglas Moore Jr.*

Brings tears to my eyes
Feeling empty and alone
Because I lost my Love Jones

If she only knew
The dreams I could see
For her and me
Then maybe she would understand
How much I loved being her man
And that she is the only lady 4 me

Even if her love does not come back to me
She loved me enough
To last an eternity
But I just wish she knew
I'd do anything
To bring things back to
What they were meant to be

## MONEY CHANGES THINGS

It's strange to me
How your mood has flipped
Changing from that rude attitude
To being all friendly to me
Thinking I don't know the real reason
In your change of demeanor

Stop trying to play me for a fool
What did you think I would forget
When I tried to get close to you
You turned around and said
You only like thugs
No corporate proper speaking brotha
Was good enough
To show you love

I don't know who told you
My pockets run deep now

*Douglas Moore Jr.*

But you need to stop trying
To get my money like it's the lottery
By saying how my personality
And body resemble the guy
You visualize in your dreams

Your game ain't working on me one bit
I've figured out your whole script
I refuse to give in
So don't bother reading it to me
I'm not feeling what you have to say

Because when I wanted to be your man
You said to move out of the way
For me to understand it is not in the plans
To give me a chance

So how could you expect me to
Forget about those days
And want to be with you today

# "AND I PICKED UP THE PHONE –PART 2"

I remember like it was yesterday
I was sleeping so peacefully
And the phone suddenly rang
Curious to see who
Wanted to speak to me
I picked up the phone
And it was her
The one who took her love away
From me so abruptly

But to my surprise

She had something to say
About how she hopes
It's not too late
To pick up the shattered pieces
Of our relationship that
Should have never ended

*Douglas Moore Jr.*

And mend the divided fence
That came between her and me

I'm lost for words

As she kept trying to explain
How she regretted the mistake
Of pushing my love away
And she prayed
The pain and strain
That was caused by her flaw
Would not put a permanent dent
In fixing our relationship

Confused and surprised

I quickly realize
I need to take some time
To make up my mind
To see if I can put behind
All that has happened
And be back with
The love of my life

I explain to her
That I never lost hope
I just kept the faith
That one day
Her love would return
To it's rightful owner

Which is me
The one she is meant to be with
Through thick and thin
So there are no reservations
On my part
About letting her back
In my heart

# WANT ME BACK

You said that you want me back
Since you now regret your past decision
Of taking for granted what we had
By putting our love to the side
So you could be with some thug
Who refused to show you love
Saw you as his flavor of the month

And when he got tired of spending your checks
Having your heart on lock
He pushed you away
Like yesterday's news
Because he wants someone new on the block
Now feeling you're blue and used
Wanting to see if I'm still feeling you

All I got to say is
You thought you could treat me so cold

*Douglas Moore Jr.*

By trying to break my heart and soul
Like you have that kind of control
Of what my future holds

Well the second you left my life
Yeah I spent some time crying
I thought I was my fault
Like I did something wrong
For your love to be suddenly gone

But one day I finally realized
It was your fault not mine
And with a blink of an eye
I could easily see that
I was crazy to actually believe
A good lady could not see
A good man like me is one to keep

And obviously you could not understand
What you really had until
It was way too late
To fix what necessarily did not have to break

## SO DO I

So do I release myself
From the feelings
That continues to overcome me
Since you decided to
Push our love to the side
And cut me
Out of your life
Without truly explaining why
You want to move on
While having feelings
That are so strong

I keep finding myself
Trying to justify loving you
Is still right
Even though the pain
You have caused me
Makes my tears

*Douglas Moore Jr.*

Come down like rain
And I tend to frown
When I reminisce about the days
Of you being around
Because I'm pretending
As if your love
Is still in my grips

So do I conclude like you
Our love has died
And it was right for the time
By saying we are no good apart
Or do I go with my heart
That somewhere inside of you
The love still flows through

And you realize the fact
This feeling is the best
You've ever had
That no other guy
Can love you
Quite like I

# NO LOVE FOR THE GAMES

I need to get out in the open
The lack of love I possess
For those who have the audacity
To test the minds
Of people with kind hearts
Who put all their time searching
For the love
Which brings joy to their life

But instead wind up feeling torn apart
Because someone who failed
To keep it real from the start

They all want to claim
To take no part in playing the games
But seem to be the main players
When it comes to leading a person on
Until she gets what she desires

And then without hesitating
Decides who will be her next prey
Because treating a guy trife
Seems to keep her going in life

Since I understand how the games operate
I am left with a sense of bitterness
Not knowing why it has to be like this
And I feel the need to hesitate
About letting a lady get close to me

I need to take the time to see
If she is just using this opportunity
To relieve her own miseries
Make her interesting stories in her diary
Which only makes it clear to me
I can never love the games
Because they cause nothing but pain

# CHAPTER 6: THE LOVE IS OVER

# PULL AWAY

I think about what you did
After ending our relationship
You chose to be with another guy
Who refused to treat you right
Decided to break your heart
Because he had no love for you
From the start
And all I'm left to say is

Why did you pull away from me
When I showed you the love
You said you had dreams of
And that once it became a reality
We became so close to each other
That pulling away
Was something I thought could never be

I notice the pain he left
By looking at your face

*Douglas Moore Jr.*

I can only imagine
The numerous times
He made you cry
By playing with your mind
A woman of your beautiful nature
Should not be treated so bad
And all I'm left to say is

Did you ever think about the times
When I held you tight
In the middle of the night
And said I'll never pull way
Because my love for you
Grows more each passing day
Even in the moments of despair
My love will continue to be there
So why did you pull away

# BEST EFFORT

I gave my best effort
To love you
While all you continued to do
Was be difficult to me
For no apparent reason

It's crazy that
I allowed this ordeal
To go on for so long
But I had such strong feelings for you
That it got me to conceal
Realizing how you were not being real

I thought my best effort
Was enough
To keep me in your heart
But I guess I was wrong
Since it seems moving on

*Douglas Moore Jr.*

Is the best way to go on

I put all of my heart into this
Hoping that you would eventually see
You and me are meant to be
Even through all the problems
That seemed to put a dent
In our relationship
I still believed everything could be solved

In the end
I had to realize
I needed to stop pretending
This broken love
That once used to be
All I thought of
Is not what it used to be
I gave my best effort
To make this work
But I still ended up hurt

## SOUR HONEY

I remember the days
I used to lick my lips
In anticipation of tasting
The honey her body generated
And once I got to fulfill my crave
Not one drop of her honey
Would go to waste

Her honey was so sweet
It would easily
Bring me to my feet
And before I went down
To put my hands on her hips
I'd make sure no other bees
Were around my honey
So I could tasted that unique flavor
Set for me to savor
Because no other honey

*Douglas Moore Jr.*

Could compare to hers

All of a sudden
She stopped showing me love
And I could sense
The change of moods
Mostly the rude attitude
That made me realize
Around her hive
It consists of so many lies
That I want no part of
In my life

The sweet taste of her honey
That used to fulfill me
Has now gone sour
And I am no longer hungry
For that bitter honey
Which is the last thing
I'd ever want to devour

# FADING AWAY

I thought you were the one for me
Until you started playing games
That made me start to realize
Things are not the same

Because you barely smile
Or look me in the face
When you have things to say
And I'm getting this feeling
Our love could come to an end
Which might not even allow us
To stay as friends

Doesn't seem too long ago
We reminisced about the first time
You told me I'm the only guy
Who stays on your mind

*Douglas Moore Jr.*

And your thighs divide only for me
Because I satisfy you
With the mental and physical
Love that feels so original to you
And you told me to never let go
But you are the one losing the grip
On the love that was on your finger tips

I wish there was a way
For me to take away
The stress and pain
That is putting our love to the test
Slowly fading it away each day

But the dilemma can be put to rest
If you can look me in the eyes
Tell me what's on your mind
So we can shed some light
On the differences
Between you and I

# IN THE SHADOWS

I stand in the shadows all alone
Because of the cold way
She decided to take her love away
And suddenly this scene
That I wished was a bad dream
Quickly became reality to me

She was the one I gave all my love to
Until she said out of the blue
We were through
It's not because I did anything wrong
She just feels we do not belong together
And that she is going back to the guy
Who cheated on her all the time
And when I asked her why
She is leaving me for his lies and deceit
She said that he is the love of her life

*Douglas Moore Jr.*

So now I'm stuck in the shadows
Completely out of the mix
Wondering why this
Had to happen to me
Convincing myself it's not my fault
Her love is long gone
And I should not get caught up
In trying to make one last attempt
To talk her out of being with him

# TEMPORARY FLING

Before she came into my life
I had a cold-hearted demeanor
Never let a lady get so close to me
That she could know what I'm thinking

But then one day out of nowhere
She came into my site
And I could feel this change coming over me
Something I never felt before

I could see myself opening the door to my heart
To her from the start
Without even blinking an eye
Not worrying if I catch feelings

My vision is all blurred
All I can do is think of her
And the second I got too caught up in the moment

*Douglas Moore Jr.*

She choose to leave me alone
Because all she wanted was a temporary fling
That was not supposed to mean anything

I'd be lying if I told her that
I no longer care for her
Even though she chose to hurt me
And keep what we had as a temporary fling
Instead of seeing if there was a possibility
Of something real between her and me

But I must confess I learned my lesson
To never to wear my heart on my sleeve
Because once I started catching feelings
Reality ended my dream
All I had was a temporary fling
That really had no future possibilities

# I GOTTA LET GO

I have to let go of what is not true
The possibility of it being you and me
I know it will be better this way
Because all I have ever wanted
Was for you to spend all of your days
With the person who helps you believe
That true love is something
You can achieve
By opening your eyes
Putting behind the past
In order to discover
A love that will last

Even though I am not your love
You will always be
The one I am thinking of
The feelings I have
Will never leave my heart

*Douglas Moore Jr.*

But I realize the bond
That we started
Has fallen apart

I wish things did not turn out this way
However in this situation
There is not much I can do or say
Except keep the faith
Hope things will turn out ok

All of the memories
Will always stay close to me
Even though I am left without
That special girl to care about
I understand there is only once choice
One I have tried to avoid
As difficult as it may be
I need to step to the side
I gotta let go

# CROSSED PATHS

The other night I ran into my ex lady
Not knowing whether if I should say anything
If she was to come approach me
And all the following thoughts came into my head
Before I could put the situation to rest

Things with her and me did not end on good terms
She proved by her lies and deceit
That showed her true colors
I deserved to love someone other than her

At first I believed she was the type of lady
I used to dream would come my way
Intelligent, Beautiful, and Honest
So when she would come home stressed
I used to run her bubble baths
Put a smile on her face so she would laugh

*Douglas Moore Jr.*

She used to say to me
I was all she needed to get by
The one she could love the rest of her life
Through the roughest of times
And she wanted me to stick by her side
Because a good man is hard to find
And I fill her heart just right

When those words came through my ears
I thought I had it all
And it would get better over the years
But I could not of been more wrong

She started to take for granted
The love I gave her each day
Like it would never pass away
If I felt like she did not know my worth
And it hurt to see how she suddenly changed
So I realized things would not be the same
Between me and her

So when her and I crossed paths
Yeah I looked her straight in the eyes
No words came to mind
I knew the best thing for me to do
Was to keep on walking forward
Because looking back brings back the painful past
Of why her and I did not last

# LEAVE ME ALONE

I can't believe that
I fell into your trap
For so long
That I actually thought
The way you treated me
Was the way
It was supposed to be

Until one day I finally realized
I am way too strong
To allow anyone to do me wrong anymore
So our love is out the door

Now I can say so long
To your lies and deceit
That caused me so much stress
Put me to the test
Until I had enough of your mess

*Douglas Moore Jr.*

To finally say
Leave me alone

I don't want any phone calls
Notes or letters
Saying you can love me better
Because you had your time
To realize my worth
Instead you chose
To treat me like dirt

So leave me alone
Put this whole thing in the past
It was never strong enough to last
From the 2$^{nd}$ you lied to my face
My love for you slowly faded away
Each passing day

Stop trying to pretend
We can make amends
One day be friends at the end
After the unnecessary pain
You brought my way

Now I'm at the phase
I can easily walk away
Go on that search
For that special girl
Who deserves to be in my world

## About the Author

Doug is a 25 year old Finance/Budget Analyst who resides in New Jersey. Doug graduated from Belleville High School and went on to the Richard Stockton College, where in May 2001, He earned his Bachelor's degree in Accounting. During his time at Stockton, in the Spring of 1999, He joined Phi Beta Sigma Fraternity Inc. and he participated in raising money for children with birth defects. volunteered on Thanksgiving at hospitals, provided career-oriented workshops for Stockton students and spent time assisting at local food banks.

Over the last few years, Doug was able to develop as a writer and decided it was time he pursued his dream of writing a book and through 1stbooks, his vision has now become a reality. In addition, Doug enjoys working out, listening to music, bowling, going to the movies and comedy clubs, along with just being around positive people who enjoy life to the fullest.

Doug hopes that all the readers of "Fresh Thoughts" will come away with a positive feeling that no matter how difficult the challenges socially and personally that life can bring, there is always a light at the end of the tunnel for happiness.